The DREAM TRAVELER'S QUEST

-2-
THE CURSE
OF SHADOWMAN

D1529340

TED DEKKER
KARA DEKKER

ISBN 978-0-9968124-7-4

Theo stared out the window in first period language arts while Mrs. Baily rambled on about the Revolutionary War and how George Washington led the country out from underneath British rule. Normally, he would be enthralled with this lesson. He loved American history and Mrs. Baily's assignment to write a fictional story set in the time period sounded like fun. But today he was stuck in his head.

Two weeks had passed since he'd entered the book and found the first seal. Two weeks and not a word. Talya had promised to send a sign.

When the sign came, he could go back into the other world to find the second seal. But Talya hadn't said what that sign would be, only that he would know when it came. Maybe it had come and he'd missed it. Maybe it was here right now and he wasn't seeing it.

Or maybe he'd dreamed the whole thing up.

The idea was unsettling. What if his experience in the other world hadn't been real? But the white circle on his arm was real. So the other world had to be real too.

"The answer, Theo?" Mrs. Baily's voice interrupted his doubts.

"What?"

"What is the answer?"

The whole class was staring at him. He had no idea what Mrs. Baily had asked.

He cleared his throat. "Sorry. Can you repeat the question?"

Mrs. Baily crossed her arms and took a deep breath, disappointed. He knew he'd been distracted the past two weeks. Mrs. Baily had clearly noticed.

"What was the name of George Washington's secretary of the treasury?"

He knew this one.

"Alexander Hamilton," he answered, glad for his dad's obsession with the Broadway musical based around the life of Hamilton.

"Correct. Alexander Hamilton was not only the secretary of the treasury, but also a writer. Hamilton wrote . . ."

Mrs. Baily continued to talk, but his mind drifted to the question of whether or not he'd missed Talya's sign. If so, he would never get the next seal. If he didn't get the rest of the seals, he would become the same fearful boy who'd been so afraid of the dark that he couldn't sleep without a nightlight. He didn't want to be afraid. He really liked his new unafraid-of-the-dark self and was happy leaving the superhero nightlight stuffed behind his socks in the top drawer of his dresser.

But it was more than that. It was Elyon. And he wanted to go back.

He swallowed and sat back, anxious.

The bell rang loudly overhead and jerked him from his thoughts. He threw his binder and pencil in his backpack and stood from his desk. As he headed toward the door, Mrs. Baily's voice stopped his exit.

"Theo, can you come here for a second?"

He sighed and spun on his heel to face his teacher. She stood in front of him, smiling. He knew she was about to ask him why he'd been so distracted lately.

"Are you okay, Theo? Is there something you need to talk about?"

"No . . . I mean, I don't need to talk about anything. I'm fine."

"You sure? It's not like you to zone out. Once or twice I get, but it's been a reoccurring thing these past few weeks. You're not in trouble or anything; I just want to make sure everything's all right."

"I'm sure. Thanks, Mrs. Baily. Everything's okay. I've just had my mind on other things."

She looked at him, concerned. The silence made him uncomfortable.

"Can I head to lunch now?" he finally asked.

"Yes, you *may*."

He turned, ready to leave this awkward situation.

"Oh wait!"

He reluctantly looked over his shoulder.

"Will you take this to your father?" She picked up a coffee mug from her desk with the words "Best Dad Ever" scribbled on the front. He recognized it as the Father's Day gift he had given his dad years ago. He and his mom had made it at one of those pottery shops the year before she died.

"He was kind enough to let me borrow it for the morning. I left my coffee sitting on the counter at home. The coffee in the lounge isn't the best, but it had to do. I can't start my day without a cup of joe."

"I'll go ahead and take it to him. See you tomorrow." Theo took the mug from Mrs. Bailey, finally managing to get to the hallway.

He figured now was as good a time as any to find his dad. His dad was probably in his classroom where he stayed most of the time, avoiding Principal

Brox, who was as much a bully as his son Asher.

Today the quickest route would be to cut through the old elementary school playground. He exited the double doors leading to the outside world and shivered.

Who has kids eat lunch outside in the winter?

The yard was already filled with yelling students enjoying their freedom despite the cold. Since the cafeteria was being fumigated, for what he didn't want to know, students were encouraged to either bring a sack lunch or purchase a sack lunch from the school. Lunch was earlier than usual—too early—and outside for the rest of the week, messing up their class schedules.

On days like this when their regular school day was interrupted by field trips, assemblies, or infestations in the cafeteria, he typically spent his time on the platform between the monkey bars and the metal slide of the old wooden playground. Once the school system had finished building the new elementary school across town—making room in the former building for more sixth-, seventh-, and eighth-graders—the playground had been abandoned, but not by Theo or Danny. Although they shared this hideaway, they each respected the other's wish to be left alone.

Danny usually kept to himself. Theo wondered if Danny's blindness was the reason he didn't talk to anyone.

And I will blind you over and over again.

The Shataiki's words replayed in his head, but he quickly pushed them away, remembering the truth. He was the son of Elyon, and Elyon could not be threatened.

He checked his hideaway. Danny was there—alone. It was only a matter of time before Whitmore Christian Middle would tear down their one place of escape.

As he passed the swings, dodging feet, he dared a quick glance over to where Annelee White normally sat. She was there, the prettiest girl in the whole school. He'd thought so since she walked into his kindergarten class as the new girl.

For the past six years he'd watched her, wishing he had the courage to tell her how pretty she was or at least talk to her. But he knew that day would never come. She was way out of his league.

Annelee sat on the picnic tables with a few of her friends, reading some teen magazine with the image on the cover of a girl gripping an ice cream cone with one hand, holding a tube of lipstick in the other.

She laughed.

He loved her laugh. It wasn't dainty; rather, it was full and contagious. Her blonde hair seemed to glow in the morning sunlight. And her eyes were deep green, like the lake where he'd met Elyon. She suddenly looked his way.

Was she looking at him? Of course not. Why would she?

He quickly lowered his head and picked up his pace. Distracted, he ran straight into another student. Before he knew it, he was shoved to the frozen ground. The coffee cup rolled out of his hands.

"Watch it, maggot!"

He would know the sound of Asher Brox's voice anywhere. Asher singled him out and made an example of him every opportunity he got. A chill ran down Theo's back.

Theo snatched up the coffee cup, held it close, and looked up to see Asher and three of his goon squad standing over him, scoffing.

"World's best dad," Asher snickered. "Such a baby. Going to give that to your pathetic father?"

He spat in Theo's direction and then moved on, eyes on another prize: Annelee. The girls closed their magazine and ceased their giggling, watching Asher's approach.

"Hey there, Annelee," Asher said, pulling up in

front of her. "I was thinking you could go to the dance with me tonight."

The Whitmore Christian Middle Snow Ball was a big deal at their school, especially to the sixth-graders who were now old enough to be put in a sweaty gymnasium with awful music and dance around for two hours while their parents watched from the sidelines.

He hated the idea. But even more, he hated hearing Asher ask Annelee. Theo didn't know how to talk to her much less ask her to go to some silly dance, but she absolutely couldn't go to the dance with Asher!

"Anyone but Asher," he whispered, slowly pushing himself to his feet.

"Thanks, but no. I'm going with my friends."

"No?" Asher snapped.

"Sorry."

"You're saying no to me? You do know who I am, right?"

"Everyone knows who you are," she said. "I bet your dad would let you stay after school and help us decorate if you want."

Her friends giggled. Theo and most likely everyone watching the exchange between the two knew Asher would never agree.

Asher stared in disbelief and then frowned. "Whatever. I didn't want to go with you anyway. I mean, have you looked in the mirror lately? What do you think, guys?"

"My grandma is better looking than her," one sneered.

"Uh, how do you spell 'ugly'? I think it starts with an *Anne* and ends with a *lee*," another joined in.

Theo watched as tears flowed down her cheeks. Asher and his goons cackled like a pack of hyenas. The rest of the students were silent, holding their breath, with eyes locked on Annelee.

She jumped off the picnic table and ran toward the school.

He wanted to run after her to make sure she was okay, but he didn't have the nerve. She probably didn't even want his help. Why would she want help from someone she didn't know existed? Besides, Asher would probably kill him if he saw him going after her.

Theo headed in the opposite direction, toward the school and his dad's classroom.

He stepped through the door, took a seat at one of the desks, and pulled out his peanut butter and jelly sandwich. "Hey, Dad!"

"Hey, buddy. No eating outside today?"

"Nah. Mrs. Baily gave me your mug."

"Ah, yes. She didn't have one."

"Yeah, she told me," he said and then sighed.

"What's up with you lately, Theodore? You seem more down than usual."

"Asher made Annelee cry on the playground. He basically called her ugly in front of everyone." He took a bite of his sandwich. Strawberry. His dad always made his favorite.

"Oh, no. I have her older sister in class this year. Sweet girls. Maybe you should teach her how we deal with bullies. Just stay invisible. Avoid trouble."

"Yeah . . . maybe." He bit his lip. Maybe this was the time to talk to his dad about Elyon and how Elyon had taught him that he didn't have to be afraid. He had wanted to tell him so many times these past two weeks, but once again, he held back.

"Hey, so I have a joke you'll like," his dad said. He loved jokes. "What kind of car does a Jedi drive?"

Before Theo could respond, his right shoulder began to burn. He looked down at the sleeve of his black T-shirt. His heart jumped. Light was shining through his shirt—the circle on his arm was glowing brightly.

How? Was this the sign?

When he looked up to see if his dad had noticed,

Stokes, the fluffy white Roush from the other world, was sitting on his dad's desk with a giant smile spread across his fuzzy face. Theo blinked, stunned.

"Theo!"

"Stokes?"

"What?" his dad said. "No, that's not it; the answer is *Toyoda*. Get it, cause Yoda was a Jedi?"

Theo glanced at his dad—he couldn't see Stokes! He forced a chuckle at the joke. "Good one, Dad."

"Thanks for the courtesy laugh."

Stokes surveyed the room, mouth gaping. "This is amazing! I've never been to this world." Stokes pointed to a stapler. "What is that?"

Theo shook his head at Stokes.

"Son, what are you looking at?"

"Uh . . . nothing. Nothing at all. I think I'm actually going to head back out for lunch. Thanks for the talk, Dad!"

"Are you sure? It's a bit chilly today. Button your coat."

"What is this?" Stokes asked, poking at a role of tape and then at some paper clips. "Shiny sticks?"

"I really should be going, Dad." He hoped Stokes would pick up the hint. They needed to leave, but the Roush was too distracted by all of this world's gadgets.

"I want to look at all this stuff. So pretty, so smooth. What's this?" He sniffed a bottle of glue and frowned.

Theo cleared his throat. "I'm leaving now."

"Fine. I'll come." Stokes flew past him, plopped to the floor, and waddled out into the hallway.

"Bye, Dad."

"Are you sure you're not coming down with something?" his dad asked.

"I'm fine. Promise."

Theo hurried into the hallway to catch up with Stokes. The hall was empty, thank goodness—empty except for Stokes, who'd found an open locker and was halfway inside digging through it.

"What's in this smelly bag?"

He ran to the white Roush. "You can't go through peoples' lockers!" Theo pulled at the fluffy body, tripped on his heel, and sent them both tumbling to the floor.

He looked up and down the hallway for signs of life. Still empty. He scrambled to his feet, grabbed Stokes's wing, and pulled him toward the closest classroom door, hoping it was unoccupied.

"Easy, easy, you're going to pull my wing off," Stokes objected.

"We have to hide!" Theo barged into the room, saw it was vacant, and pulled Stokes in after him.

He dropped to one knee and threw his arms around his friend. "I missed you!"

"I've missed you too, Theo!"

"You're here! I didn't know you could cross over into this world! Why *are* you here?"

"I've come to tell you who to bring with you on the next quest. Talya was going to send Gabil, but I begged him to send me. I'm a mighty warrior, as you know. And you are my charge, so it only makes sense. I must get you back as soon as possible."

Theo stood, scratching his head. "But how did you get here?"

"A special fruit Talya gave me! When I ate it, I was brought here. I have another fruit to get back."

"A fruit? You ate a fruit and it brought you over?"

"Of course! There are many kinds of mysterious fruits. There is one special fruit that you eat and you don't dream. You know how you came home last time when you slept? Well, if you had eaten that fruit in my world, you would have stayed there. Very special, yes?"

Special? Yes. Makes sense? No.

"So who's the person I need to bring with me?"

"Her name is . . . Oh, my goodness, what was it again?"

"Her? A girl?"

"Good thing Michal wrote it down for me," Stokes said, rummaging through the little brown satchel he wore across his chest. He pulled out a piece of paper and unrolled it. "Oh yes, her name is Annelee!"

"Annelee? Are you sure that's what it says?"

"Yes! Annelee White! Let's go get her." Without waiting, Stokes bounded to the door, pulled it wide, and entered the hall.

"Wait, Stokes," Theo cried, stumbling after the Roush. "It can't be Annelee! I can't even talk to her!"

"Have no fear!" Stokes took to the air and flew down the hall. "I, Stokes, the mighty warrior of Elyon, protector of Theo, will tell you what to say."

Of all the people in the school, why did it have to be Annelee White?

Theo ran after Stokes as he flew through the school. The sound of his squeaking Converse tennis shoes echoed through the deserted halls.

"Slow down! Do you even know what Annelee looks like?"

Stokes pulled up mid-flight, turned to him, and then settled on the floor. "Actually, I have no idea what she looks like. She is a human girl, right? We aren't looking for an animal or something, right?"

"Yes, she's a human girl. I know her, but—"

"Oh good!"

"We can't ask Annelee to come with us. She'll never talk to me."

"Don't be silly. You're a mighty warrior just like me! Besides, there is no choice in the matter. It has to be her. Talya made that very clear."

Theo frowned, nerves rattled. The thought of talking to Annelee made his stomach knot, let alone asking her to come with him to another world through a book with his invisible talking bat.

"You don't understand. I—"

The bell rang, cutting him off.

Stokes spun around. "What was that? Is that your battle alarm? Are we about to fight someone?" He threw up his fists.

"No, that's called a school bell. It tells kids when each class period ends."

"Period? What does period mean?"

"Never mind."

Students rushed through the outside doors and flooded the hallway. Stokes lifted to the air and watched curiously.

"Wow! They all look like you. Cute."

He ignored the Roush, knowing they needed to get away from all these students.

"We need to make a plan to talk to Annelee."

A few questioning eyes glanced curiously at Theo. *They think I'm talking to myself.*

"I'm, uh, practicing my lines . . . for the play," he said, blurting out the first thing that came to mind. There was no play.

Theo ignored their awkward stares, walking casually down the hallway as if he didn't have a white bat waddling behind him. He led Stokes into the art room, knowing there were no art classes for the day because of lunch's altered schedule. Shutting the door behind them. he let out a sigh of relief.

"Okay, so how do we get Annelee into the other world?"

Stokes jumped up on a table and fiddled with a paintbrush. "She has to put a drop of her blood into *The Book of History*, like you did."

"So not only do I have to convince her to come with me to the library, but I need to persuade her to cut her finger. Great, this is going to be a piece of cake." He climbed up on a stool next to Stokes and dropped his head down on the tabletop.

"Have no fear! Should we go grab her now?"

"No!" Theo lifted his head. "She'll be in her next class by now."

"Oh," Stokes said, disappointed.

"But now that I think about it, there's this silly dance tonight. Annelee's part of the decorating team. They're staying after school. I guess I can ask my dad if I can stay and help. That will give us a chance to talk to her."

"*You* will talk to her. Remember, I'm invisible."

Theo gulped. "Guess that's our plan then?"

Stokes snapped one finger into the air. "A perfect plan!"

"I better get to my next class. You just wait in here. Stay out of trouble. Promise?"

"But of course!"

"I'll come get you in a little bit."

***

Praying that Stokes hadn't caused a disturbance, Theo finished the school day and convinced his dad that he wanted to stay after school to make decorations for the school dance.

He sat on the glossy wood floor, cutting out snowflakes and watching Annelee across the room. Stokes flew around the gymnasium, touching everything, amazed at the things Theo saw every day—the basketball hoop, the overhead lights, the bleachers, the students.

Theo nibbled at his lip, trying to figure out the best way to approach Annelee. She sat on the bleachers studying what appeared to be a playlist of songs that would pump through the speakers that evening. She had pulled her blonde hair into a ponytail and had changed into a yellow-striped dress. Her eyes were red from the confrontation at lunch, which made him hate Asher Brox even more.

Stokes plopped down next to him, breathing heavily. "Well? Talya said we must hurry."

"I know. I'm about to go," he whispered.

"What are these?" Stokes asked, picking up one of the paper snowflakes.

"Snowflakes."

"Snow? This doesn't look like a snowflake to me. It's paper."

Theo had to admit, they weren't the best. "My mind is on other things right now."

"Right! Then you must hurry."

He put down his half-cut snowflake and headed across the gym, gathering as much bravery as he could muster. He stopped five feet from Annelee, heart in his throat.

She looked up at him and smiled. "Do you need help with something?"

"Um . . . no. I . . . um . . . " He froze.

"Be brave, mighty warrior!" Stokes cried, swooping in to take a spot on the bleachers just above Annelee. "She is so pretty!"

"Yes?" Annelee asked curiously.

"Hi, my name's Theo."

"I know. Theo Dunnery, right?"

She knows my name?

"Right . . . right. Theo. So, I need to show you something in the library."

"The library? What's in the library?"

"Well, it's—"

"Sorry. I have a lot of work to do."

He cleared his throat and took a deep breath. "Please, it's important. I'll tell you why on our way there."

"Tell me why now."

"It's kind of hard to tell you without showing you. But, you see, there's a special book in the library."

"A book? Maybe later. I really don't have time."

"If you come now, I promise to make a thousand snowflakes."

"We don't need a thousand snowflakes, even if you could make them. Maybe tomorrow."

"Tell her it will change her life!" Stokes said, hopping down next to her. "And the dance."

"Um . . . It will change the dance!"

"And her life!" Stokes chimed in.

"And your life. It will change your life. And it can't wait until tomorrow. We have to go right now."

Annelee pursed her lips and stared at him. "Fine. Five minutes. That's all you get. I don't see how a book can change anything."

"Thank you, Annelee."

He exited the gym with Annelee on his heels.

"You did it!" Stokes shouted as he flew circles around them. "Maybe you should tell her about me!"

Theo shook his head, eying Stokes.

"So what is this book?" Annelee asked.

"It's called *The Book of History,* I think, but it's not a history book. It's about this mysterious place where this boy has to find these seals of truth, and he sometimes needs help from other people to find them."

"So you're taking me to the library to see a fictional adventure book? How's that going to change the dance?"

"You'll see," he said, pushing open the library doors.

Mrs. Friend, the librarian, sat behind the circulation desk. "Annelee! I'm glad you stopped by. The winter edition of *Style Teen* arrived yesterday. I shelved it in the periodicals. You know where to go."

She blushed. "Thank you, Mrs. Friend."

Mrs. Friend leaned toward Theo. "Are you back to have a look at that special book you were showing me a couple weeks ago?"

"Yes, ma'am. Actually, I was wondering if I could borrow the key to the room to show Annelee."

"Well, sure! I was just finishing some things up for the day, but I'm sure I can find something to do while you're up there. The book's right where we left it."

Mrs. Friend lifted the key from around her neck and handed it to him.

He thanked her and made his way up the stairs. "This way."

"You have so many books here!" Stokes said, following Theo and Annelee to the second floor. "So many stories. I love this place."

Theo stopped at the door and placed the key in the lock. The door clicked. He pushed it open. Annelee peeked over his shoulder to see inside the tiny dark room.

"The book's in there?"

"Yeah, it's special, like I said." He reached around the corner, flipped on the light, and entered the room.

Annelee followed, curiously looking around the dusty space.

"Remember, she has to bleed on one of the pages. Maybe poke her. I'll go find something poky." Stokes flew from the room.

The idea of sticking Annelee with something sharp was unsettling, but he didn't have any other ideas.

"All right, so where is this book?" she asked, hands on her hips.

"Here." He found the bookcase where Mrs. Friend had placed the old book and pulled it off the shelf. It was large and heavy, with a worn leather cover. The moment he held it in his hands, the tattoo on his shoulder began to heat up. His pulse quickened as his excitement grew. It was as if the book knew who was holding it!

He laid the book on the floor and opened it to the same page he'd used to cross into the other world.

"It doesn't have any words," Annelee said.

Theo rubbed his finger across the splotch of dried blood that colored the blank page.

"The story I told you about in this book is real. It leads to another world. In the other world I'm on a quest to find five seals. I already have the first one." He squirmed with each unbelievable word. "The five seals will change everything. You're supposed to help me find the next one."

She glared at him as if he'd lost his mind.

"I know that sounds crazy."

"You aren't serious, are you? There's no way you can be serious. I've gotta go."

Stokes flew into the room and dropped a thumbtack into Theo's hand.

"No, wait! Please. Let me show you."

He grabbed Annelee's hand and pricked her finger over the book.

"Ouch!" She jerked away, but as she did a tiny droplet of her blood landed on the page.

"Why did you do that?" she cried. "You've lost your mind!"

"She will see soon!" Stokes said. He took a bite from the fruit he was holding. And with that single bite, he vanished.

"I'm sorry. I needed your blood, and I knew you wouldn't give it if I asked."

"Are you crazy or something? You cut me!" She backed away from him. "I'm going to report this—" But then the book began to glow and she stopped.

His pulse accelerated. It was working!

The glow flooded out of the book and surrounded them in warm light.

Chapter 2

"What's happening?" she cried, rushing up to him.

The light twirled around them and the room began to fade from sight. All he could see was the white light.

"Theo? Where are you?"

"It's okay! Don't be afraid!"

The light around them dimmed to a low glow. Then, they were gone.

Theo's hands pressed against the warm sand. A cool breeze brushed his skin, and a sweet scent perfumed the air around him. He was back.

He opened his eyes slowly, allowing them to adjust to the brightness of the sun. He lifted his body off the warm ground and sprang to his feet. A smile formed across his face as he jumped around in excitement.

"Yes!" he squealed. "We did it! I'm back."

He saw the staff Elyon had given him lying on the ground. And beside it, a leather strap. He looped the sling over his chest and gripped the wood. It felt good to have the staff back in his hands.

What adventure awaits us next, old friend?

He wielded the staff, striking an imaginary Shataiki upside the head.

"What's happening?" a scared voice croaked beside him.

Annelee sat up on her knees, looking around at a world he already knew but that was totally foreign to her. She looked terrified.

He remembered the feeling.

"Don't be afraid. This is the world I told you about."

"This can't be real! This can't be happening!"

"But it is real, and it is happening. Just like I said!"

She closed her eyes, her breathing heavy. She wasn't taking this well, and Theo didn't really know what to do to help her calm down.

He hesitantly placed his hand on her shoulder. "Annelee?"

She pulled away from him and stood to her feet. "Why are we in a desert? I don't understand why we're in a desert. We were just in the school. I must be dreaming. I'm dreaming. This is a dream."

"I know how you're feeling. The first time I came here I was alone and scared and had no idea what was happening. But everything's going to be okay."

"What did you do?" she cried, spinning toward him. "This can't be real! We aren't in the library anymore?"

"No, we're still there, but asleep, I think. But we're

also here, in our dreams, sort of. At least that's how I think it works."

"So we're asleep in the library right now?"

"I think so."

"I don't believe you. Take me home! Wake me up! I don't care, just get me back!"

This wasn't going how he hoped. "I can't."

"Why not?"

"I need your help."

"Oh, right, something about a seal. That's absurd!"

She'd been listening. That was encouraging.

"Yes! I told you, I have a special quest. I have to find the five Seals of Truth that will save me from my fears. I discovered the first seal. Look!" He lifted his shirtsleeve to show her the glowing white circle imprinted on his shoulder. "The first seal."

Annelee brushed her finger over the circle and then jerked away. "It's hot!"

Theo lowered his sleeve, proud of his accomplishment. "When we find the second seal, we can go home."

She surveyed the desert. "Not that I understand a bit of this, or that I believe you, but let's just say this isn't a dream and this second seal can get me home. Why me? Why do you need *my* help?"

"I don't really know."

She threw her hands up in the air. "You brought me here, and you don't know?"

"Talya said you had to come with me."

"And who's Talya?"

"He's a mystic, sort of my teacher. He told me I would need help finding the next four seals, that someone from my world would be chosen to help me. I guess you were chosen. That's why I had to get you to the library and get your blood into the book. It's what makes the book work."

Annelee placed her hands over her face and shook her head. He didn't blame her. It was a lot to take in.

She lowered her hands. "I still don't understand."

"Let's find Talya. He has a way with words."

But he didn't know how to find Talya or how to get out of the desert. Where was Stokes when he needed him?

Theo scratched his head. In the distance, cliffs rose from the desert. It seemed like their best option.

"Follow me," he said with as much confidence as he could fake. He hoped he looked like he knew what he was doing.

They began their trek across the sands with Annelee reluctantly following and asking a hundred questions. "Who lives here? What do they look like?

Explain these seals again. Are we lost? How long will we be gone? Are you sure this isn't a dream? How did you find the first seal?"

He did his best to answer, but every explanation he gave sounded absurd, so he finally told her to ask Talya.

If only the Roush were here. Why hadn't they found them yet? Surely Stokes had told them they'd crossed over, unless something had gone wrong.

Theo knew that if they didn't find Talya soon, Annelee would plop down on the sand and sit there until she woke up. He needed her. He needed her to help him find the second seal.

She'd finally fallen silent.

Theo just hoped Annelee didn't completely hate him. Maybe if she could see him use the staff . . .

His attention wandered to thoughts of the adventure awaiting them. Would he have the chance to see Elyon again? He desperately hoped so. Would he even see the Roush? Would he encounter the Shataiki? The memory of those nasty bats made him cringe.

"Theo?"

He turned back and saw she'd stopped. "Yes?"

"What's that?"

She pointed to the sand fifty feet away. A large shadow of a bat darkened the sand.

"Shataiki!"

He grabbed Annelee's hand and ran toward an outcropping of rock to their right. He might have looked up to see the Shataiki above them, but he dared not. And he didn't want her to see them either. Looking into their eyes could be dangerous. He should know.

"Hurry!"

Their feet pounded against the sand. The sound of the Shataiki's flapping wings became louder as the shadow drew near. There was more than one. Maybe dozens!

They reached the rock. He pulled her behind it, slammed his back against the stone, and tried to quiet his breathing.

"What's happening?" she cried.

He put his hand over her mouth and motioned for silence. She nodded, and he pulled his hand away.

"What's happening?" she whispered.

"Shataiki. The evil black bats I told you about."

"You never told me about . . . evil bats!"

He was sure he had, but then again, there was a lot he hadn't told her—like the time he'd been captured by the Shataiki.

"Let's just say, they're not our friends. Don't move."

Annelee's eyes grew wide. Her fingers dug into his arm as she clung to him for protection.

But the sound of flapping wings had stopped—which meant one of two things. The Shataiki had either flown by, or they'd landed and were creeping toward them.

Theo pressed his head against the rock. He took a deep breath and mustered up his courage.

You can do this. You're the son of Elyon.

With his staff held tightly in his hands, he peeked around the corner of the rock. There sat three white bats with giant green eyes.

Relief washed over him. He ran toward the Roush and threw his arms around the first of them.

"Oh my!" Michal said, returning his embrace.

"We missed you, Theo," Gabil said.

"Where have you been? I thought you were Shataiki!"

"How silly and insulting," Gabil laughed. "I look nothing like those ugly things."

"I had to find them first, and then we had to find you," Stokes said.

"Well, I'm glad you did."

"Where is Annelee?"

Annelee came out from behind the rock, shaking. "Send me back! Wake me up!" She backed up, staring at the Roush, frightened. "Wake me up right now!"

"I'm guessing this is her?" Gabil said, waddling toward her. "There is no cause to be afraid unless you're a Shataiki in disguise, in which case you'd better run for your life."

She grabbed a handful of sand and flung it at Gabil. "Stay away!"

The sand caught Gabil full in the face. He sputtered, swatting at his nose.

She flung another handful of sand. Gabil stumbled, tripped over his own feet, and landed on his tail.

Theo knew she was frightened, but that didn't keep him from laughing. Michal and Stokes quickly joined him, their laughter pouring out of them as they watched Gabil struggling to get to his feet while wiping his face.

She grabbed another fistful of sand.

"Annelee, stop," Theo said. "These are my friends, not the Shataiki."

She lowered her arm, blinking. "I don't care. I want to go home."

"But you may, my dear," Michal said, "just as soon as you find yourself. I am Michal, this is Stokes, and the one you attacked is Gabil. We are Roush, not Shataiki, and we are here to help you find yourself."

"What do you mean, *find myself*?" she demanded. "I'm right here."

"You'll see, my dear," the Roush said. "You'll see soon enough."

Annelee inched over to Theo, frowning. "I don't like this. I don't like it one bit."

He leaned into her. "But aren't you a bit curious?"

"Don't be ridiculous. A talking bat is telling me to find myself!"

He shrugged. "Okay, okay. But just so you know, these three talking bats are the bravest and most loyal friends anyone could have. They helped me on my last quest."

"And saved him many times!" Stokes said.

"Oh . . ." Annelee looked over at Gabil, back on his feet and smiling sheepishly. "Sorry for the sand."

"Gabil, did you just let a little girl best you with sand?" Michal asked.

"I could have most certainly taken her down with one move, but I don't hurt humans. Plus, she's a lady, not a little girl."

"The master of the Roush fighting art got put in his place by a lady," Michal said. He took Annelee's hand and bowed. "Thank you, my dearest."

A hint of a smile crossed Annelee's face.

Gabil pushed Michal out of the way, took her hand, and bowed as well. "No harm done here, sweet lady. Nice to meet you. Gabil at your service."

"Sorry, again." She turned to Michal with an arched eyebrow. "So, other than finding myself, can *you* tell me why I'm here? Apparently, Theo doesn't know."

"That's not fair!" he said, irritated by her accusation.

Michal cleared his throat. "Talya will answer your questions better than I can."

"That's what I've heard. I can't wait for this Talya person to tell me why Theo Dunnery forced me to come to the desert." She glared at Theo. "I hope it's worth it."

"It is," Michal said. "The next seal is as much for you to find as for Theo to find."

"Me?"

"With Theo's help, of course. It deals with your biggest fear."

"What fear?"

"That's for Talya to explain. But I will tell you that even the seal Theo has can easily be lost if you don't find the next soon. So I suggest we get going. Talya is waiting for us."

Michal turned and waddled away.

Theo knew Annelee was as clueless as he had been on his first day in the other world. He could see it in the way she studied the Roush and watched the sky for the Shataiki. She was more concerned about her safety than him losing his seal. But he knew what losing the seal would mean. All of his fear would return.

He couldn't let that happen.

"**S**o, the white bats are Roush, and there are black bats called Shataiki?" Annelee asked.

"Yes, but we Roush are beautiful, and they are not," Gabil replied.

Theo had to bite his tongue to keep from piping in. He knew all of this, and he wanted to let Annelee know he knew. He'd told her about the book and the other world. She knew he'd been here. So why was she more interested in the Roush's answers than his?

"And Talya is a wizard, and this is all magic?"

"No, Talya is a mystic, and this isn't magic," Theo answered for Gabil.

"Well, sorry if I don't know everything yet, your royal highness. If I remember correctly, you need me here, and I don't want to be here, so you better be nicer to me if you want my help." She looked back at Gabil. "So, how can you talk?"

What kind of question is that?

He rolled his eyes. He didn't want to upset her any more than he already had. This quest would be impossible without her.

They left the desert, traveling through a forest Theo didn't remember.

"Michal? Why aren't we going through the Roush village to get to Mount Veritas?"

"We're taking a more direct path."

"I scouted it out!" Stokes chimed in.

"Yes, Stokes found it. Time is short. You must reach the doors as quickly as possible. Also, if we were to go through the village, too many Roush would delay us, eager to see a human again. They've all heard by now."

"What doors?" Annelee asked.

"You'll see when we reach the mountain," Theo said. "It's hard to describe."

"Try anyway," she demanded. "Just tell me what to expect."

"Okay. There are five of them and they're different colors with symbols, like on my shoulder, but not everyone can open them."

She sighed, frustrated. "Maybe someone else should try to explain them."

"If you wait, you'll see for yourself," he mumbled.

Gabil wobbled up beside Michal. "This seems to be taking longer than I remember. I thought it was supposed to be a more direct route."

"Yes, well, we were flying last time. Stokes, are you sure this is right?"

"Are you trying to go toward the mountain?" a tiny voice said from behind them.

The travelers spun around, startled. Theo reached behind his back and grabbed his staff, readying himself to fight.

But there was no sign of anyone.

Suddenly, a young girl with gray eyes stepped out from behind a large tree, staring at them with great excitement. Her skin was almost as gray, cracked like broken concrete.

"What's that smell?" Annelee whispered.

Theo inhaled and coughed. Annelee was right. The stench was rotten, awful.

"She's Horde!" Michal said, surprised.

"My name is Maya. I'm sorry if I frightened you, but I can help you find your way. My mother and I have lived in these woods for a while now."

"Why aren't you in one of the Horde cities?" Gabil asked.

"We were banished," she said, gracefully walking closer. "But Talya taught us the ways of Elyon."

Annelee backed away as she approached, so Maya stopped.

But Theo was intrigued. "You know Talya?"

She grinned. "Yes! He is a very wise man!"

"Stokes, what is Horde?" he whispered.

"Horde is what my people are called," Maya said. "Our skin is covered in a disease that causes us much pain. Horde believe Elyon is evil, but I know differently. Do you know him?"

"I do!" The mention of Elyon reminded him of the reason he'd returned.

"When the Horde bathe in the Red Lakes, they encounter Elyon and that experience heals them of many issues," Gabil said, "including their skin disease."

"But if you believe in Elyon, why are you still Horde?" Theo asked. "Why haven't you been to the Red Lakes to heal yourself?"

"Talya is teaching me and my mother that we are beautiful. Even though our skin may not be, our beauty lies inside us."

"You *chose* to stay like that for a lesson?" Annelee asked.

Maya nodded sheepishly.

"I don't think I could do that. I wouldn't be able to look in the mirror . . ." She put a strand of loose hair behind her ear. "It's hard enough as it is."

She's afraid.

Theo looked up at her, shocked. Did Annelee not know how beautiful she was? He had spent most of his life in fear and knew it when he saw it. Annelee was afraid. Could a person be afraid of not looking pretty enough? It didn't make sense, but she was definitely afraid of something.

He shook the assumption away and faced little Maya again. "It's very nice to meet you, Maya. I do think we need some help. My Roush friends are kind of lost."

"I've never seen a Roush before," she said, staring at Gabil. "You're just as cute as Talya said."

"He said that? I would have said fierce." Gabil flashed a grin.

Stokes waddled up to her. "I've never seen Horde before, but I'm glad to meet you, the sweetest Horde alive, surely." He bowed.

Maya giggled and returned the bow.

"I suppose I got us lost," Stokes said sheepishly. "So if you know the way . . ."

"Of course! Follow me!"

They followed Maya through the forest. Theo's mind buzzed with new information—red lakes and Horde. There were so many questions he wanted to ask, but he didn't know how to ask them. And he didn't want to look clueless in front of Annelee.

Annelee stayed at the far back of the group. She had pulled the neck of her dress up over her mouth and nose.

He slowed down, allowing her to catch up with him. "Hey, I know she smells, but you don't have to be rude."

"I'm not being rude! Besides, it's not the smell." She frowned.

"What is it then? Her looks?"

Silence.

His mouth fell open. He couldn't believe it. "It's because you think she's ugly!"

She shushed him. "I never said that."

"But you thought it."

"It's not like you don't think it too."

She was right. He had thought it. Maya certainly wouldn't be called pretty in the other world. At school, everyone would stay as far away as possible.

They came to the edge of the mountain where a long flight of steps rose to a cavern above them.

"This is where I say goodbye," Maya said. "I think you will find Talya at the top."

"Will we see you again?" he asked.

He hoped so.

"Only Elyon knows." And with that she headed into the forest and vanished from sight.

"Well, let's start climbing, I guess," Stokes said.

The group traveled in silence. Theo couldn't stop thinking of Maya and the Horde. He guessed Annelee's mind was on the same thing. But where he was curious, she was clearly bothered.

He wondered how she'd do with the rest of the journey. He knew nothing of what was behind the second door. What if she was too weak to find the second seal?

The stairs ended at the large cavern, and inside were the two giant wooden doors he'd entered through last time.

Annelee gasped. "Wow!"

"Wait until you see what's behind them," he said, encouraged by her excitement.

Michal knocked three times as he'd done before. The doors swung open. The group entered, following the torch-lit tunnel until they came to the room with the five colored doors. On each side of the doors hung unlit torches.

Theo touched his shoulder: white, like the circle above the first door. He'd been afraid when he walked through that door.

Talya stood to their left, dressed in a long robe,

hands behind his back. His beard was as white as his cloak and his eyes a brilliant green.

He lowered his arms and winked. "Welcome back, young Theo." He offered Annelee a raised brow and a warm smile. "And it's so nice to see you here, Miss Annelee. I'm glad you came. My name is Talya."

She stared, at a loss for words.

"Not to worry, my dear. I do not bite."

"No. I'm sure you don't," she stammered. "Sorry, I . . . You make it sound like it was my choice to come."

Talya chuckled. "But you did choose it, my dear, just not in the way you think you did. At any rate, you will soon thank Theo for doing as I asked. If you want to blame anyone, blame me. I told him to bring you here."

"Why me?"

"You'll see."

A silence passed over the group as if Talya were allowing her a moment to think.

"Well then, we should go through the second door, right?" Stokes asked.

"Not so fast, my brave little Roush. Theo and Annelee must go through the door alone. No Roush friends this time."

"What?" Theo did not like this at all. There was no way he could survive without the three Roush!

"Have faith in yourself." Talya clapped and immediately the two torches next to the second door sparked to life—the green door.

Annelee flinched and grabbed Theo's hand.

"This will be a great adventure, Theo!" Stokes said. "I will be waiting for you. Remember everything I taught you and you will be fine."

"Everything you taught him?" Michal asked.

Stokes hadn't really taught him anything. If anything, the young Roush was as much a student as Theo.

"Don't fear, Annelee," Gabil said with a wink. "Theo is a master with his staff, if I do say so myself."

"It is time," Talya said.

"Aren't there other instructions?" Theo asked frantically. "Last time you told me where to go and what to do."

Talya faced Annelee and looked deep into her eyes. "When you learn to love the one you first despised, you will find the seal and go back home. It's the only instruction you need."

A familiar feeling bubbled in Theo's belly. Understanding that the mission depended on Annelee and Annelee alone made him uneasy. So then, what was his role?

"You will support her with all you know," Talya said, as if he'd heard Theo's thoughts . . . again.

Theo nodded at Talya, gave Annelee's hand a squeeze, and then walked toward the door, guiding her forward. "It's okay. Follow me."

He placed his free hand on the handle, turned the knob and cracked the door a smidge. The door sprang wide open on its own accord. Warm light filled the doorway.

"I'm afraid," she said as the light crackled and swirled in front of them.

"Everything will be okay. I promise." A promise he wasn't sure about. Not at all. "Come on."

The moment he stepped forward, the light began to pull them both through the door. Then they were floating in a tunnel of beautiful, warm light.

"Theo!" she cried.

But no sooner than they were floating, they were through. The light vanished, leaving them in a stinking, dimly lit space with a dirt floor.

He spun around. The doorway they'd come through was gone.

"What just happened?" Annelee twisted around, confused. "Where are we?"

"I don't know. Last time it dropped me off in a forest. This is new to me."

Fear crept into Theo. Where were they?

Theo squinted, adjusting to the dim light. The room was empty except for simple wooden shelves lining three of the four stone walls.

"I think we're in some sort of pantry, maybe part of a house or something."

"Why does it smell so bad?" Annelee asked, stepping up beside him.

"I don't know."

He moved over to the shelf closest to him, stacked with what appeared to be bags of grain or food of some kind. He leaned in, sniffed, and then backed away quickly.

"Found out why," he said, covering his nose with his arm. "Whatever it is, it's rotten."

The sound of boots clacking across a stone floor echoed through the room. Someone was coming toward them!

He grabbed Annelee and pulled her between two of the shelves. He didn't know if they were in the company of a friend or an enemy, and he wasn't eager to find out.

They held their breath as the handle turned and the door swung open. Light flooded the room paired with a familiar, unpleasant odor—the same scent that had followed little Maya.

A large man with cracked gray skin and hair braided into thick dreadlocks stood in the doorway, frowning. Horde. And from the looks of it, not a very nice Horde.

Theo could hear Annelee's breathing quicken. She was afraid. He knew it would be only seconds until they were found. He slowly pulled his staff from its sling and held it in front of him.

The man stomped into the room. "Hello? I heard you. If this is one of the Hutchen brothers again, I told you, no more food!"

The man was moving straight for them. Theo gripped the staff with one hand and gently pushed back on Annelee with the other.

The man crept closer.

Theo held his breath.

Two dark-gray eyes locked on them. Theo swung his staff high, striking the man's jaw with a *crack*.

The man jerked back, startled. Theo saw their opening and took off running with Annelee stumbling behind.

They tore through the door and found themselves in a small house. But he didn't stop to figure out which way to go—he just ran.

They rounded a corner, found themselves in what appeared to be a kitchen, and came to a screeching stop.

Where's the door?

He spun around to find another way, but the man was standing in the hall, scowling.

Theo threw his staff with all his might, but this time the man was ready. The man snatched it from the air, tossed it to the ground, and was on them before they could move. He grabbed them tightly by their shoulders at arms length and looked them over.

"Well, by the fangs of Teeleh, what do we have here? Albino spies?" The man spat on the ground. "Have they fallen so low that they send their children to come into our camps to gather information? Doesn't surprise me."

Theo wanted to say that they weren't spies and that he didn't know what Albinos were, but his mouth wouldn't move.

"Why don't I take you two to where you belong," the man growled, dragging them behind him.

Theo fought and kicked until he realized that the man's grip was too strong. He glanced over to Annelee, catching her eye. He wished he hadn't. He could see her panic. Why would Talya send them here? He feared for her even more than he feared for his own safety.

The man pulled them to the door and into a bustling street market where the people—assuming Horde really were people—traded, argued, played, and moved about. They all looked like Maya and the man who had them: men, women, and children, all with the same smelly, flaking, gray skin and dark eyes.

They had to be in one of the Horde cities Maya talked about. A chill washed down his spine. This wasn't good. It wasn't good at all!

The Horde went about their business as the man hauled them down the street, but that didn't mean Theo and Annelee passed unnoticed.

Seeing two kids with smooth skin was clearly a rare thing in this city. But, as soon as they passed, the people returned to their business. They weren't a threat to the Horde, only a curiosity.

The man pulled them past a group of Horde children, some who appeared to be their age, playing a game like soccer. As the three passed by, the children stopped their play, staring.

What would it be like to live looking like them? He couldn't help but wonder.

He was brought out of his thoughts when one of the children spat in his direction. The rest of the children followed suit.

"Albinos!" one of them called.

Albinos. He and Annelee were Albinos, and they weren't well liked here.

The man dragged them into a stone building and led them down a dank passageway. This place was much darker than the pantry of rotting food. They turned down another passage. Rooms with iron doors and bars for windows lined the rock walls.

A dungeon.

The man opened one of the doors and shoved Annelee and Theo inside. "One of our nicest rooms. Enjoy." He slammed the door closed, leaving them in the cold, damp cell.

"This isn't good," Annelee said. Her voice was thin and shaky.

Theo ran his hands up and down the bars. He pushed, then pulled. They wouldn't budge.

The cell was almost completely dark. The only light trickled through the barred window-like opening at the top of the wall. When night came, there would be no more light. *Darkness*. The familiar fear clawed deeper into his memory.

He closed his eyes tightly and whispered to himself, "Elyon is with me. Nothing can hurt Elyon, so nothing can hurt me. I fear nothing." But the fear didn't leave. He was no longer certain of his protection.

"What are you saying?" Annelee asked.

"Just trying to remember my last seal." He sat down on the dirt floor. "I'm so sorry. I don't know what's happening. This isn't like last time. Bringing you here was a mistake."

Silence engulfed the room. He didn't know what else to say to her, so he sat quietly, fidgeting with the laces of his Converse.

Annelee let out a sigh and slid down the wall across from him. "We just need to figure out what to do. How about your Roush friends? What would they do if they were here?"

"Not get captured, for one," he said, frustrated. "I don't know. Figure out a way to escape? But I don't see how."

"You have the first seal on your arm, right? Does it have a power or something?"

Theo leaned his head against the wall. It was hard to translate into words what he'd felt when he received the first seal.

"It's a truth that gives me power."

"What kind of power?"

"Well . . ." It didn't look like they were going anywhere fast, so he decide to start from the beginning. "When I was here last time, I was captured by the Shataiki."

"The bad bats, right?" She was listening this time.

"They put a fear in me, a fear of Elyon. They told me he was cruel and that he punished those who failed him. They convinced me he was a monster. But all of that went away when I met him. He's the opposite of fear."

"Really? How so?"

Theo took a deep breath and pulled up his sleeve.

The white circle glowed on his arm. "White," he said aloud. "Elyon is the light. Nothing can threaten him."

"I don't understand."

"He showed me who he really is. Nothing can hurt him; nothing can disappoint him. That's the first seal. He showed me that he loved me no matter what I did, and that I don't have to fear because he's always with me and I'm always with him. I know it sounds silly, but I was filled with so much courage and . . ." The truth felt weird to say, especially in front of a girl. "Love."

"So . . ." She paused. "Who is he? Who's Elyon?"

Theo closed his eyes, thinking of how many times he'd asked the Roush the same question. "I don't think I could tell you who he is really. I don't think I'd do him justice. In our world, we call him God."

He paused as the same confidence and wonder he'd experienced with the boy on the beach edged back into his mind.

"As a friend once said to me, he's indescribable. If you ever meet him, you'll know."

He could barely see Annelee's face in the dark cell. But he had her thinking. He knew it, because his own fear had eased, and she could surely hear that in his voice.

Simply talking about Elyon had a way of bringing

a calming peace. He let that peace settle over them.

"So, what's the second seal?"

"I don't know," he said. "That's why you're here."

"Not sure I'll be much help," she said, looking away. "I don't even understand what Talya said to me."

He remembered. "When you love the one you first despised, you will find the seal. Or something like that."

"Right. But I don't despise anyone, except maybe Asher."

He wasn't exactly a fan of Asher's either, but surely Talya hadn't meant Asher. He didn't know what else to say, so the silence returned. They leaned against the dungeon walls and waited in the dark.

No one came; nothing changed. They were just two kids wondering if they had been left to rot.

In that empty silence, Annelee started humming. She rocked back and forth, holding her arms over the striped dress covering her legs.

"Annelee? Are you okay?"

"Yes, of course. I finally decided that this is all a dream. There's absolutely nothing to be afraid of. Soon I'll wake up and laugh about how Theo Dunnery was in my dreams."

"This isn't a dream," he said. He was irritated

with her doubt, especially after all he had told her about Elyon. But at the same time, he knew how she felt. How many times had he thought the same thing before realizing the truth? "This is real."

"I don't believe you," she snapped. "I mean, it makes no sense. Even your seals don't make sense. If you learned that nothing can hurt you, and this man named Elyon told you that nothing could hurt you, then why are you still so afraid?"

"I'm not . . . I'm just . . ."

"Just what? See, you don't even know. Elyon sounds just like the stories I heard in church as a little girl. He promises to be there but never shows up when you need him. Where is he now? Why hasn't he saved us?"

"Annelee . . ." What else could he say to make her believe?

"Forget it. I know I'm dreaming, so just go away."

Theo felt defeated. He'd tried to explain Elyon but there was no way she could understand the first seal like he did. Or maybe he didn't know Elyon as well as he thought he did. This new question came crashing in with another dose of fear.

The door squeaked open. His heart beat wildly. The same man who'd tossed them in the dungeon stood in the doorway. A second man stood behind him, holding a torch.

"You two must be special 'cause they want to see you," the Horde man scoffed.

"Wake up," Annelee muttered as if to herself. "This is all a dream. Wake up."

"What's up with her?" the man said with a nod toward Annelee. He clamped chains down around Theo's wrists. The memory of the Shataiki ropes binding him came back—the black fog. He tried to shake away the fear.

The man yanked Annelee to her feet and shackled her wrists.

"Don't dally," the other man snarled. "They're waiting."

Theo wondered who *they* were and what *they* wanted. Whatever it was, it couldn't be good.

The men led them up a flight of stairs to a chamber where four Horde sat behind a long stone table. Others gathered around them, waiting in silence. They were in a courtroom or something.

Annelee and Theo were directed to the middle of the room.

"Face the council."

The man at the center of the table glared at them, lips flat. A gray robe hung loose over his frail frame. His dreadlocks were tied behind his head, making his forehead appear large and menacing.

Slowly, a thin, mocking grin spread over his horrid face.

Theo wanted to tell Annelee that everything would be okay, that Elyon would save them. But in that moment, he wasn't so sure.

"Welcome to your trial, my little putrid Albinos," the man hissed.

Theo's stomach tightened as the man's gray eyes drilled into him. The hiss of his voice echoed in Theo's head. Sweat beaded around his forehead. Like the black fog, his fear began to smother him.

The man rose from his chair and placed his palms on the stone table in front of him. His gaze skipped back and forth between Annelee and Theo, as if trying to sum them up.

"My name is Eleazar Vanstone, chief justice of the court. I've been told you two are Albino spies who have come into our city to extract our secrets. Is this true?"

"No," Theo squeaked.

"No? Really? Well, I've never heard of an Albino casually strolling into a Horde city for fun. Have you, Zeke?" He glanced at the man who had captured Theo and Annelee.

"No, sir."

Theo cleared his throat. "It wasn't our choice to come here. We . . . well . . ."

He tried to think of the best way to say how they got to this world, but he was at a loss for words. He couldn't say they walked through a magical door that sent them to Zeke's pantry. Could he?

But Annelee spoke first. "We went through a door of light that sucked us in and dropped us in that . . . room."

"I see." Eleazar stood straight. "A door of light brought you here. Well, why didn't you just say so? Zeke, it was a door of light that brought them."

A scattering of snickers spread across the onlookers.

"That's right," she snapped. "We didn't want to come here; we were forced to. But this isn't real. None of it's real. I'm dreaming."

"Dreaming. I understand now." Eleazar's smirk slowly turned sour. He slammed his palms down on the stone table. "Do you think we are idiots, you fool?"

The slap of flesh on stone echoed through the room. Annelee jumped and her lip quivered. She was terrified. So was Theo.

"Now, once more," Eleazar said. "Why are you here? It seems odd, even for diseased Albinos to send children to do their dirty work."

"I don't know who the Albinos are," Theo said. "We were with the Roush, and . . ."

He was cut off by another round of chuckles echoing through the room.

"Roush?" Eleazar scoffed. "You must have a large imagination. Roush don't exist."

"But they do! I know them well!"

"We've had enough. No more talk of magical doors and mythical creatures." Eleazar pursed his lips. "If you can give no logical explanation for your presence, then we will be glad to execute you as the spies you are."

Annelee gasped beside him. Tears flowed down her face.

"Or . . . we could use you as test subjects for Ba'al's potion." Eleazar sat back in his seat. "Our priest is close to curing the Albino disease. The Red Lakes have poisoned you, but with our cure, all Albinos can be healed and brought under Horde rule."

"We don't have a disease!" she cried out. "You do! Can't you smell it?"

"I can smell your rotting flesh, little child." Eleazar spat to one side. "Elyon has put so many lies into your Albino heads. I feel pity for you."

"Elyon isn't a liar," Theo said with an authority he didn't know he could muster.

Eleazar clicked his tongue and shook his head. "Poor child, already lost. Well, the choice is yours. Take the potion and turn Horde, or die. Rather simple if I do say myself."

Annelee sat like a statue, too terrified to speak. Anger flushed Theo's face. Die? Could this really be happening?

The judge's eyebrow arched. "Perhaps execution is the best—"

"We'll take the potion," Theo interrupted.

The judge frowned. "Fair enough. Zeke, inform Ba'al. The potion will be administered here, in this very courtroom."

Zeke dipped his head and left the room.

Theo didn't know how to feel. He avoided looking at Annelee as they awaited their fate. How could Talya do this to them? Talya had sent them to this fate without any instruction. He could feel the heat on his cheeks as the thought ran through his mind.

Zeke came back into the room flanked by two other men. One was clearly a guard. The other could've walked straight out of one of Theo's childhood nightmares.

His skin clung to his bones. He was much thinner than the other Horde Theo had met. His fingernails were long and he wore a hood that cast his face in shadows. He almost looked more Albino and less

Horde than the others, but in a twisted, disturbing way.

An air of dread came over the room as the wretched man passed. The council and the watchers bowed.

"Ba'al, High Priest," Eleazar said with reverence, "be pleased with the subjects we have taken for your most noble cause."

Theo dared not connect with the priest's empty eyes, so he kept his head bowed, not out of reverence, but out of fear.

"They will do," Ba'al hissed.

"Let all who are here be witness to the new age of Horde," Eleazar announced. "May the Red Lakes no longer hold power over us. May—"

"Silence, you fool," Ba'al interrupted.

With one hand clenched at his side and the other extended, Ba'al stepped up and lifted Theo's chin with his long finger. There was something about staring into the priest's eyes that made him feel lightheaded.

The man dropped Theo's chin and pointed a boney finger at Annelee. "You," he hissed. "You will drink first."

Ba'al opened his fist and held out a glass bottle to Annelee.

"Drink."

With hands trembling, she took the bottle. She closed her eyes, placed the rim of the bottle to her lips, and tipped it back.

"Good girl."

She handed the bottle back to Ba'al, eyes wide.

Theo watched as her eyelids fluttered. She started to shake. Her body suddenly went limp, and she crashed to the floor.

"Annelee?" Theo started for her but Zeke jerked him back. Annelee's body lay in a heap, breathing heavily. She was alive. But that was hardly a consolation.

An icy hand gripped his chin, turning his face away from Annelee and toward Ba'al's dreadful glare. Hot breath washed over his face. It was all he could do to keep himself from gagging at the putrid stench.

"Drink." Ba'al pressed the bottle into Theo's hand.

He held the glass tightly, lifted the bottle to his quivering lips, and allowed the bitter, black liquid to flow into his mouth. The world around him seemed to slow as he choked it down.

Almost immediately, his mind began to fog. The world tipped and a great heaviness settled over him.

Theo collapsed to the floor and the room went black.

Theo lay on a cold surface, head pounding.

He pushed himself to a sitting position and placed his hands on his head, trying to stop the world as it spun around him. He found it hard to keep his eyes open. They burned. So did every part of his body. His skin felt like it was on fire.

An awful smell accompanied the pain—the smell of rotting eggs and sour milk.

The potion!

A part of him was too afraid to look at his skin, but he couldn't stop himself. His skin was gray and diseased—he could feel the dry cracks covering his entire body. Seeing it, the pain increased and the smell overwhelmed him.

He was Horde. He was Horde, which meant . . .

Theo scanned the room and found Annelee

crumpled in the corner. He scrambled over to her, ignoring the pain in his joints.

Her skin matched his. The potion had turned them both Horde!

Annelee lay still, but her chest rose and fell. Her blonde hair lay messily across her cheek. He brushed it back. Her face, though gray and cracked, was still beautiful. He doubted she would see it that way.

He leaned against the wall next to her and tried to make sense of it all. Why hadn't they awakened in the library after they were knocked out? Last time he'd fallen asleep here, he had woken up in the other world.

Then he recalled the fruit Stokes claimed kept a person from dreaming and traveling. Maybe it was inside the black potion they'd taken.

What had he done? Would he ever get back?

His mind drifted to Elyon and the seals. He didn't know what he was supposed to learn this time. How could he or Annelee accomplish anything locked up in this dungeon, covered in this wretched disease?

If only Talya had told him something—where to go, what he was looking for, anything that would help. But he'd only told Annelee that they would find the seal when Annelee loved what she first despised.

She remained asleep. Once she woke up and

saw what they'd become, she would lose it, and he wouldn't blame her.

He'd forced her into this world. Now they were in a dark dungeon, covered in this painful skin. This wasn't Talya's fault—it was entirely his fault.

"Theo?" Annelee moaned.

He jumped to his feet and helped her up.

"Ow . . . my skin . . . "

"I know. Me too."

She gasped and backed away from him in horror, eyes on his skin.

"What . . . what happened?"

"It was the potion . . . in the bottle."

She stared down at her cracked, gray arms. "No. No! It can't be true."

"I'm so sorry."

"This can't be right. We can't look like those horrible things! It's just a bad dream, right?"

Annelee rubbed her hand across her arm and then pulled it away. Tears slipped down her diseased face.

He hated that he'd made her cry so much. He hated that he'd put her in so much pain. He hated a lot of things right now.

"I'll figure out a way to fix this. I don't know how right now, but I'm sure there's a way." He didn't believe his own words.

She wiped her tears with the back of her arm. "You had better fix this," she snapped, sinking to the floor. "You've turned me into a monster!"

Theo settled next to her, dejected and at a loss for words.

"I look disgusting. It's not like I was pretty or anything, but now I'm hideous." A new round of tears flooded her eyes. She lowered her head into her hands.

She really didn't know how beautiful she was. It made no sense. Everyone at school thought she was pretty. He'd wanted to tell her for a long time, since that day she walked into their kindergarten class.

"That's not true," he said. "I've always thought you were pretty."

"Were? And now?"

He bit his lip, embarrassed. "Now too."

"Thanks, but you don't have to lie. We both know I look disgusting."

"I'm not lying. I think you're the most beautiful girl I've ever seen. Even now, covered in Horde skin, you're beautiful."

He could feel his cheeks redden, but hopefully the gray skin kept the red hidden.

Annelee looked up at him, her brow scrunched. "Really?"

"Yes."

He could tell by how she absently studied the cell wall that she was thinking about something, maybe what he'd said. He only wished she could see herself the way he saw her.

"*Psst.*"

Theo jerked his head up toward the sound. There, on the other side of the cell bars, stood a Horde girl, staring at them.

"Maya!" Theo leaped to his feet.

"Talya sent me," Maya said." I've come to rescue you. He said I'm safe because no one will look twice at a little Horde girl."

"Rescue us? How?"

Maya pulled out a pair of keys and wiggled them in front of the door.

"Where did you get those?" Annelee asked, stepping up to the bars.

"I'm very sneaky." Maya beamed.

She put the key in the door. The lock clicked and the door swung slowly outward. Theo and Annelee rushed from their dark prison.

"We must be quiet," Maya said. "The guard on duty is sleeping. I slipped some Rugeta fruit into his drink, and it can make you very sleepy. But he won't be asleep for long, so we must hurry."

A surge of energy raced through Theo—he was ready to run if it came to that.

"Put these on." Maya handed them Horde tunics. They quickly slipped them over their heads. "Now that you're Horde, no one will pay us any mind. We are just three Horde children going home." She grinned widely. "Ready?"

"Ready," Annelee whispered, breathless.

"Ready," Theo said.

Maya turned, and then she was off with Annelee and Theo on her heels. They passed the sleeping Horde guard and exited the dungeon without being seen. It was night, and the moon shone brightly in the dark sky over the great Horde city. He was glad to see some light again.

Maya slipped down a narrow alley blocked by a gate.

"You guys can climb, right?" She made her way to the other side with ease.

Theo helped Annelee up and then climbed up and over. A sense of courage overcame him. Maya pulled him to the wall with a finger pressed against her lips. Two men stood at the exit of the alley—guards.

There was no telling what Ba'al would do to them or Maya if they were caught escaping. He inched along the wall behind Maya, saying quiet prayers that the men wouldn't venture farther down the ally. There was a laugh, then a chuckle, and the guards moved on.

Maya held up her hand. "Wait."

Brave girl.

She ran down the alley, peeking around the corners to see if their path was clear. Then she waved them forward. They followed her down the alley and out into an empty street.

Maya led them past a Horde building and then another. "It's not much farther. Just over that wall."

In the near distance a tall stone wall marked the edge of the city. Behind them, they could hear voices and the sound of boots pounding on the hard ground.

They know we escaped. "Go!"

The trio ran. The wall was in sight—just a few more feet. Once there, Theo boosted Maya and then Annelee.

Annelee leaned back over the wall's edge. "Come on! Grab my hand!"

Theo looked back. Shadows moved in the moonlight. The Horde were coming. He reached for her hand, hauled himself over the wall, and landed on the ground in a crouch. Then they ran as fast as their legs would carry them.

But he knew that even if they could outrun the guards, they couldn't outrun what they'd become: gray, scabbed, foul-smelling Horde.

Theo ran, one foot after another, behind Maya. Annelee had fallen behind, breathing heavily, trying to keep up. Occasionally, he glanced back to see that she was okay.

They didn't stop until they reached a creek in a clearing of trees. He leaned over his knees and tried to catch this breath. Annelee plopped down next to the stream, breathing hard. Maya didn't seem to be winded at all.

He sat down on a large boulder, trying to think through their next move. Nothing was coming to him.

What now?

Annelee sat cross-legged by the edge of the stream, staring into its waters. Maya knelt down beside her. She twirled her little finger in the clear water, then left it to become still to reflect a bright moon.

"What do you see?"

"Nothing," Annelee breathed.

"Strange. I see a lot in this water. I see me, I see you, and I see Elyon."

Theo watched the Horde girl, so calm and observant, younger than both he and Annelee.

"Can I tell you what else I see?" Maya asked.

Annelee didn't respond.

"I see beauty."

"Not in me. I'm gross."

"Because of your skin?"

"Because of everything," Annelee whispered.

"Oh, I see. Yes, the skin we both own is not the most beautiful to blind eyes, to those who cannot see their true self. But do you know what Talya has taught me?" She didn't wait for Annelee to answer. "My beauty doesn't come from the outside but from the inside."

"Well, maybe my insides are as ugly as my outside." Annelee studied her reflection in the still water.

Asher had called her ugly. How could she believe him?

"Ugly and beautiful are only words. You know

what I see? I see the light of Elyon inside you. Can you see it?"

"No."

"Want to see what Elyon sees? Look closer."

Theo wanted to go over to see for himself, but he knew this was Annelee's moment, so he watched from the boulder. Annelee got on her knees and looked into the water. She stared for a few seconds and then gasped. Then she leaned closer.

No longer able to hold his curiosity in check, Theo hurried over and tried to see. But all he saw was a reflection of the moon.

"Is that me?" Annelee asked.

Maya didn't answer.

Annelee touched the water and jerked her hand away as if she'd been shocked by electricity. She slowly drew back, eyes glued to the water. Then she took a deep breath and shook her head, as if trying to understand something.

Theo wished he could hear her thoughts.

"I need a minute," Annelee said. She stood up, adjusted her tunic, and walked into the forest.

"Annelee?" he called. But she'd disappeared into the trees.

"Let her go," Maya said. "Listen to the night sounds. Do you hear the beauty? Do you hear its rhythm? It's everywhere."

He allowed the sounds singing all around him to fill his ears—the rippling of the river, the soft hush of the cool breeze, the rustling leaves that swayed above him. A deep calm settled over him.

"The light is in all of us, Theo. You will see." She closed her eyes and breathed in the sweet air. "Whenever I start to feel sorry for myself or become blind to the light, I ask Elyon to show me who I am."

Maya's words pricked at his heart. She was telling him something very important, but most of his mind was too busy worrying to hear clearly.

"I'm lost," he said. "I don't know how to find the seal. I lost my staff, and I don't know what to do."

"You will see soon," Maya said. "The skin they gave you can be taken as soon as Annelee learns her truth. But she must learn the truth in the costume she wears now."

"Costume?"

"It's what Talya calls our bodies. They're like costumes we wear while we're here, in this world. But our bodies aren't who we are. They're only what we are for a short time."

"Then who are we?"

"You'll see." Maya winked.

A wave of relief washed over him. This horrible skin could be taken away, and Maya seemed to know how. He had to tell Annelee.

Where was she, anyway? She'd been gone way too long.

"I'm going to check on Annelee."

"Don't get lost."

"I'll be right back." He took off in a jog toward the forest. "Annelee?"

Nothing.

He edged deeper into the forest. "Annelee?"

She couldn't have gone far. What made her leave? What had she seen in the water?

The forest gave way to a clearing. He saw her there, with her back toward him. But she wasn't alone.

Theo held back, heart pounding, and peered around a tree. Annelee was talking to a man, taller than her by two feet. He wore a white shirt and white pants. His hair was dark, slicked back, and his skin was glistening.

Theo felt drawn to him. Strange. It was like he somehow knew him. But something about the man didn't feel right. But it didn't stop him from wanting to trust the man.

The stranger lifted his eyes, blue in the moonlight. "Theo!"

Had they met before?

Annelee turned to him. She was beaming, happy. Something had excited her. Was it what she'd seen in the water or was it the stranger?

Theo moved out from behind the tree. "How do you know my name?"

"I know everything about you two children. I know you don't really look like the Horde who took you captive. And I know your skin is beautiful, like mine."

"How do you know all this?"

"He said he could change us to the way we were!" Annelee said excitedly. "We just have to go with him."

The man smiled at Theo with perfect white teeth and waved him closer.

Was this what Maya had spoken about? What if Elyon had sent him to help them . . . to teach Annelee and heal them?

But Maya hadn't said anything about a man.

"Annelee, can you come here? Maya told me something that—"

"Didn't you hear me? He can take this gross skin away!"

"Theo doesn't trust me yet, but he will," the man said, gaining Annelee's attention again. "Can you tell me what you saw in the water?"

"I saw a light," she said. "I saw myself through Elyon's eyes. The light was in me. It was me. I was beautiful."

"Lift up your hand, sweetheart."

Annelee did as the man instructed.

"And we know that this skin isn't beautiful, right?"

"Right."

"So, on the inside you're beautiful, but right now you're not beautiful at all. I can make you beautiful once more. I can heal you, sweetheart."

Annelee hung on the man's every word. But the more the man talked, the more Theo distrusted him. Something was off.

"Annelee, let's get back to Maya."

"But, Theo—"

"Do you trust me?"

"Yes."

"Then, please, let's go back to Maya."

The man extended his hand to Annelee. "Young Theo is lost, sweetheart, but you . . . you know the truth."

She faced him, her mouth agape as if she wanted to say something.

Theo wanted to grab her and yank her away.

"I'm sorry," she finally said. "I have to ask Maya if it's okay. She rescued us. Wait here and I'll be right back."

Theo relaxed and released the breath he had been

holding.

"Fools," the man snarled. "You aren't any more the light than I am. The Horde girl lies to you!"

The man's face twisted into a wicked frown.

"Lies! All lies! You'll see what I mean before this is over. Your time is yet to come!"

His perfect skin started to wrinkle and then fall away. Two large wings emerged from the skin and then stretched open.

Shataiki.

But not like Ruza or any of the other Shataiki. He was much larger, and his eyes shifted color from blue to gold before settling into a deep, piercing red.

The Shataiki opened its jaws and sneered.

Annelee stood still, trembling. Speechless.

Theo stepped in front of her, wishing he had his staff. A scream echoed through the trees.

Maya!

The beast cackled. "Until we meet again, my little foolish darlings." With a swoosh he swept to the night sky and was gone.

"Hurry!" Theo cried, grabbing Annelee's hand.

"What was that?"

"Shataiki . . . I think!"

They raced through the forest and into the clearing only to catch a glimpse of several Horde men riding away on horses. Maya was sitting on one of the horses, tied up and slumped over.

Annelee fell to her knees, dumbstruck. "No!"

Annelee paced back and forth in front of Theo. "We have to do something!"

"I know. I know."

"It's our fault she was taken. Why did you leave her?"

"Annelee—"

She wasn't listening. "We have to save her!"

He tried again. "Annelee—"

"What if they hurt her?"

He grabbed her by the shoulders. "We'll find her. We need to put our heads together and think this through. It won't do Maya any good if we stay here, freaking out."

She bit her lip and nodded.

He lowered his hands and took up Annelee's pacing. "Okay, well . . . we need to find our way to the city. I'm sure that's where they've taken her."

"Right."

"We'll need to find my staff first."

"What? Why?"

"Because it's special. It has power. Just trust me."

"But we don't even know where it is!" she demanded.

"I had it at Zeke's house, near where the kids were playing. We'll look there. As Maya said, we're Horde, so we won't be noticed, right?"

She hesitated. "Maybe. But how will we find Maya?"

Theo kept pacing, thinking. "Why did they take her?"

"I don't know."

He stopped and faced her. "To draw us back."

"You think?"

"Why else? They're hoping we'll go find her."

"You mean they'll be expecting us?"

"Maybe. But it also means she'll be easy to find. They *want* us to find her."

"So they can take us!"

"Which is why I need to find the staff first. Aren't you listening?"

"What good will a staff do against the Horde? You're delusional!"

Theo set his jaw. "I defeated a hundred Shataiki

with that staff! It has much more power than you've seen!"

That stopped her. He could practically see the wheels spinning behind her eyes.

He took a deep breath. "Please, I can fix this. We'll save her. And she said she knows how to get rid of the disease."

Annelee looked in the direction they'd taken Maya and then swallowed. "I think it's Maya I have to love before I can find the seal. I despised her, in a way, because of her skin. I thought she was disgusting . . . and the smell."

Theo let silence rest over them before talking.

"Well then, we have to save her."

Annelee looked back at him. "I do love her, you know."

"If you're right, it's the only way to find the second seal and get home." He paused. "Let's go."

Annelee and Theo took off under the glow of the moon, trying to recall landmarks or anything remotely familiar. They'd fled the city, following Maya, without thinking they would ever return. He wanted to ask Annelee more about Elyon and the light, but her silence told him she wasn't ready to talk. In their quiet he thought about his staff, remembering what it felt like in his hand. He saw it in his mind, pulling him closer.

It took them less than an hour to reach the city. The walls stood against the starry sky, tall and ominous as they approached and slowed, keeping a watch for any sign of guards. There were none.

Annelee stopped, hands on hips, catching her breath. She needed to rest. They both did. But Maya was on the other side of that wall.

"We'll do it like last time," he whispered. "I'll get you up and then you can help pull me up."

"What about you?"

"I climbed it once. I can climb it again."

He hoisted her up, which he found to be more difficult than he'd remembered. She pulled herself to the top and then hung over the edge, arm extended.

"Grab my hand!"

He reached up for her.

"Wait! I'm slipping!" Then she was out of sight. "Ow!"

"Annelee! Are you okay?"

No answer.

"Annelee?"

He quickly reached up for a stone jutting from the wall. He was exhausted, hungry, and distracted by the pain of his cracked skin. It took him a few tries, with many slips, but he finally found his grip. For all he knew, he could be facing the Horde guard when he landed on the other side. His mind filled with images of Annelee in their big, smelly hands. He climbed until he could maneuver his body over the edge of the wall. He let go. His feet landed hard on the ground next to Annelee.

"What took you so long?"

"Are you okay?" he asked, breathing hard.

"What? Were you worried about me?"

He ignored her sarcasm. "It's harder than it looks without help." He took a moment to catch his breath. "We need to find Zeke's house."

Theo led the way, with Annelee following tightly behind him. They moved through the city they had escaped hours before, keeping to the shadows in case a Horde guard recognized them. They were no good to Maya if they were caught.

"You see where the kids were playing?" Annelee asked. "Anything look familiar?"

"Not yet. Let's keep going."

They'd only seen these streets twice, while they were either running for their lives or being held captive. But knowing what he could do once he found his staff refueled his self-confidence.

"There!" He pointed to the alley. "We go through there!"

Keeping close to the wall, they passed through

the alley and over the gate. The prison loomed in the distance.

Annelee froze.

Theo grabbed her hand. "It'll be all right. Remember, we look like them."

"We're two children running around in the night. That doesn't make sense. What if they catch us? I can't go back there."

She was right. Despite their new appearance, it was late, and the streets were empty.

"We'll say we're lost." He squeezed her hand and guided her deeper into the city. "Over there!"

To their right was a grassy area with a net set up like a soccer goal and, beyond that, the market.

Annelee nodded. "Now, which house?"

"I think I know. What's the first thing you remember when we were taken from the house?"

"The smell."

"And?"

"The market."

They scurried over to a row of houses that opened up into the now-empty market.

Theo pointed to a house. "That's it."

"How do you know?"

"I just do."

"Wait!" Annelee grabbed him by the back of his tunic. "What if *he's* in there?"

Theo hadn't thought about that.

"Let's look inside."

He slipped over to the window, pulled himself up, and peered in through the opening. A few chairs sat next to a burning fireplace. Empty.

Then he saw it. Leaning against the wall.

"I see my staff!" He dropped down. "I'm going to crawl in and grab it. You keep watch out here."

"Be careful. If you see anyone, run!"

Theo pushed the window open, climbed through, and eased to the floor inside. He held his breath as he tiptoed across the wooden floor to reach the other side of the room. He made it to the wall and grabbed the staff, feeling its power rush through him. It was as if he and the staff were one. Had it been calling to him this whole time? Maybe that's why he had found the house so effortlessly.

With the staff in hand he felt complete again, as if a part of him that had been missing had returned.

He clambered out the window and dropped to the ground. "I found it!"

Annelee was staring across the city. "And I think I found Maya."

He followed her stare. There on the hillside was a large fire. A tall post stood next to the fire. Someone was bound to that post.

Someone small.

"Maya," Theo breathed, heart hammering in his chest.

They stood paralyzed by fear.

He couldn't think straight.

"It's a trap," he said. "They're waiting for us!"

For a moment, Annelee didn't respond. When she did, her voice was hardly more than a whisper. "Tell me again who Elyon is."

He blinked. "Elyon is the light. Nothing can threaten him."

"And you are his son? So, can anything threaten you?"

"I . . . Not really. I don't think so. But—"

"Yes or no?" she interrupted.

"No. Elyon said no."

"And Talya sent us here to find freedom from our fears, right? You trust Talya?"

"Yes," he said.

She nodded. "We have to go to her. Maya's the only one who can tell me how to get rid of this disease."

He tightened his grip on the staff. "If I'm Elyon's son, you're his daughter. So then nothing can harm you either."

"I'm already harmed," she mumbled. "You've seen my skin, right?"

"I mean, maybe your body can be, but . . ." But then he didn't know what to say, because she was right. Maybe they *could* be harmed.

"Never mind," she said. "She's my only hope."

He had nothing else to give, nothing he could put into words.

He motioned for her to follow him and took off running straight for the fire on the hill, heart pounding. With each step he prayed they weren't throwing their lives away.

As they got closer to the hill, the scene around Maya came into view, lit by the fire. Three men stood in front of Maya—Eleazar, Ba'al, and, between them, the man who'd tried to trick them at the river. He'd returned to his beautiful skin.

And he was watching them.

"Too late now," Theo breathed.

"You'd better be right about Elyon," Annelee said.

He'd been in a situation like this before, and Elyon's staff had shown its incredible power. The memory was the only thing moving his feet forward.

"My life is in your hands," she said. "If this goes badly . . ."

She didn't need to finish.

Theo ground his teeth and sprinted, screaming, straight up the hill toward the beast in disguise. He was only five paces away when he lifted his staff over his head and hurled it at the man with all of his strength.

The beast caught the staff with one hand as Theo slid to a stop, panting. He stared at the man, stunned.

The man held the staff in one fist, grinning with amusement. Annelee had stopped behind him, gasping for air.

"Did you think this was going to help you?" the man chuckled.

He twirled the staff and examined the wood.

"Pretty, pretty piece of wood. Shame it will have to be destroyed." He broke the staff over his knee and tossed the broken pieces to the side. "That, stupid boy, is what Elyon means to me."

Theo's mouth hung open. Elyon's staff lay broken in the dirt. His stomach turned inside out.

Maya was strapped to the post behind the man, mouth gagged, eyes focused on Theo. Two more posts on either side of her were empty. All three of them were going to die.

Two Horde men grabbed Annelee and tossed her to the ground next to Theo.

"It's nice that you finally joined us," the man said, glancing at Maya. "We were getting restless, weren't we, Maya?"

He faced Theo again.

"I don't think I've formally introduced myself. Some call me Vlad, but you can call me Shadow

Man. I could have taken you by force at the river, but it was important that you chose willingly, of your own free will. When you refused me in the forest, we went to plan B. And so here you are of your own choosing, like a present with a bow on top."

Shadow Man squatted down, placed his fingers on both sides of Annelee's cheeks, and turned her head to face him.

"I nearly had you, my dear. You were so eager to be rid of this horrid skin that you almost sold your soul to me. This is better though." He patted her cheek and rose. "Tie them up."

Two large hands grabbed Theo's shoulders and dragged him across the dirt. They bound him to one of the posts next to Maya.

He could hear Annelee's whimpers as they hauled her to the post on the other side of Maya. The men backed away once their deed was done, leaving the three children bound and helpless.

Shadow Man faced them as Ba'al and Eleazar watched, smirking. They were pawns in a game of evil.

"I gave you a chance, my darlings, and you failed me. Now I'm going to give you one more chance. Reject Elyon, deny him, curse the seal on your shoulder, and I'll set you all free. Refuse and you will never see the other world again."

Theo's body trembled.

"You want to know why I call myself Shadow Man?" The man moved over to Annelee and cocked his head. "Annelee? I'm asking a question."

Tears rolled down her cheeks. Shadow Man thrust his face inches from hers. "It's rude not to answer when a question is asked."

She cleared her throat. "Yes."

"That's a good girl. I'll tell you why. In your world, the Shadow Man is a boogieman that lives under your bed, hoping your feet will dangle over the side. It's a patient monster, just like me, who waits for the moment to drag you under."

He chuckled, walked over to Maya, and grazed her cheek with his thumb.

"And like that monster, I love creating fear in

children." He leaned into her and breathed in her scent. "And you three reek of fear."

A muffled whimper escaped Maya's gagged mouth.

Shadow Man turned to Theo. A crooked smile played at the edges of his mouth. Theo wanted to spit in the man's face, but he held back.

"Theo. The hero. How the mighty fall. The seal on your arm doesn't seem to be helping you any more than that pathetic staff, hmm? So what do you say? All you need to do is deny all you think you know about Elyon, including that silly seal on your arm."

It was true, the staff hadn't worked and the seal wasn't helping.

"No?" Shadow Man said. "You would rather I blind you?"

I will blind you over and over again.

Could the man really blind them?

Shadow Man stepped over to Annelee.

"What about you, princess? You don't even know Elyon. It's Theo I'm after. He's the one spreading the poison. What have you got to lose by denying Elyon? Reject him. It's just a few little words and a change of heart. If you don't, you'll be stuck here rotting in a dungeon. Poor, ugly Annelee."

But she didn't speak. She was too busy sobbing,

eyes clenched tight, terrified.

"Deny him, you little puke! Deny Elyon or I blind Theo."

She cried harder. It took all the strength Theo could muster to keep from yelling out for her to save herself.

Just say it, Annelee! Just say what he wants you to say.

But he couldn't bring himself to speak the words. He could never deny the boy who'd shown him the way past fear.

"No? Have it your way then." Shadow Man said. "Times up, sweetheart."

Two big strides and the man was standing inches from Theo's face.

Shadow Man took a deep breath and exhaled. A black mist seeped from his mouth and flowed into Theo's eyes.

Darkness.

"Deny Elyon and I will restore your sight." Shadow Man's voice echoed in the night. "Curse the seal."

Theo knew his eyes were open, but all he saw was black. Panic rushed through him. He felt absolutely helpless. How could he be blind? Talya had sent him here! Why wasn't someone here to save them?

Maya's words from earlier crossed his mind: "Whenever I start to feel sorry for myself or become blind to the light, I ask Elyon to show me who I am."

He swallowed the lump in his throat, and with his last bit of strength he cried out, "Elyon! Show me who I am!"

With those words, the darkness was gone. He found himself standing in a white desert, sand warm under his bare feet. Annelee was standing next to him.

"Annelee?"

She stared at him, dumbstruck. "Is this real?"

In answer, a giggle drifted through the air. He spun at the familiar sound. The boy. It was the boy! The boy was here somewhere! Elyon was here!

"You want to know who you are?" the boy's voice asked.

"Yes!" Theo stammered. "Yes, we do!"

"You're the light of the world," the boy said. "That's who you are."

A soft, playful growl sounded behind him.

Theo spun around to find the boy smiling at him with Judah, the lion, standing beside him. He ran to the boy and fell to his knees, overwhelmed with gratitude.

"I knew you would come! I knew it!"

The boy chuckled and ruffled Theo's hair. "Hello, Theo."

His eyes met the boy's.

The boy looked over Theo's shoulder at Annelee, who was standing behind them in shock.

"Hello, Annelee," he said.

"Hello," she said meekly.

"Do you know me?"

"I think so. You . . . you were the light in the water."

"*You* were the light in the water," the boy said. "I'm the source of that light, far greater than you, but I made you like me, in my likeness. Light. Your body is just a temporary costume, an earthen vessel."

She blinked, stunned. "Is this how you really look? A boy?"

"No. But how else would you recognize me?" He winked at Theo. "Do you want to see what I really look like?"

"Yes," both of them said, almost in unison.

The boy lifted his hand and snapped his fingers. In that instant he became light—not merely light, but a crackling light that surrounded them. It consumed the entirety of the sky, the world, the universe— infinite light.

White. Elyon is the light. The first seal.

Theo gasped and staggered back, overwhelmed by the feeling of the light. It was love. It was unspeakable power. It was . . . everything. There was no darkness, no fear, no judgment. There was just love—a love that burned up all the darkness and fear of the universe in the blink of an eye.

Elyon had showed himself to them as a boy—but no longer.

The light collapsed into the boy, and he stood on the sand, smiling.

"You like?"

Tears streamed down Annelee's cheeks. "Yes," she whispered.

"Now you try," he said to both of them.

Theo and Annelee exchanged a glance. "Us?"

"Just do what I did."

Annelee nodded at Theo. They lifted their hands and snapped their fingers.

Immediately their bodies were gone. Left were two beings of the same crackling light that had made the boy.

They didn't fill the whole universe like he had, but it was the same light, humming with power and flowing with colors—red, blue, green, gold—hundreds of brilliant colors.

Theo lifted his hand, mesmerized by the light

streaming and coiling where his fingers had been. He could see Annelee, formed like a girl, but she was now made of the same light.

And that light was beautiful. So perfect. So breathtaking.

"I am in you, and you are in me, as one," the boy said. "You're the light of the world, but you're usually blind to that light. Now you have eyes to see."

Then the light collapsed on itself, and they were once again in their old forms.

Theo stood, breathless, trembling in awe.

"I am beautiful," Annelee breathed. "It's me. It's me who I hated, not Maya. I despised myself, but now I love who I am."

Annelee was loving who she first despised. That was what Talya said must happen for them to find the second seal!

Warmth pulsed on Theo's shoulder. He reached down and lifted his shirt. A green circle now appeared inside the white one. Annelee lifted her sleeve with him. There on her arm were both the white seal and the green seal.

Light.

"Green!" he cried. "I am the light. We are the light of the world, just like Elyon!"

Annelee squealed in delight. She began to spin,

singing, "I am the light! You are the light! And such a beautiful light it is!"

She grabbed Theo by the hand and spun him. Dancing wasn't his thing, but in this moment, he didn't care. The boy laughed and joined in with the dance. Judah jumped up, shook his mane, and stomped his paws. The world around them was alive and singing in light.

Theo felt absolutely complete in this one moment. He knew it wouldn't last forever, but for now he drank in the feeling of being fearless and of swimming in the light of love.

The boy stopped and grabbed each of them by a hand. "Always remember who you are, especially when you find yourself in darkness and fear."

"We will!" Annelee said.

"Now, it's time to go."

"Please, don't leave us! We need you."

"Leave you? I've never left you. Wherever you go, I am." Then the boy winked at them and was gone.

The white sand began to fade.

Theo clasped onto Annelee's hand. "Remember who you are. You are beautiful."

"Thank you."

Suddenly he was tied to a post.

In darkness once more.

Theo knew he wasn't blind anymore. And with this revelation, the world came into sight—fire blazing, Horde glaring. Shadow Man was gloating.

"Not only are you Horde, but you're also blind," he was saying. "All you have to do is deny Elyon. I'll take all your pain away. I'll give you sight and let you return home."

Shadow Man thought he was still blind.

"Elyon can't save you," Shadow Man sneered. "I alone, the prince of blindness, can set you free. If you refuse, I'm going to throw you in a pit, blind and putrid. You'll rot there for as long as it takes you to come to your senses."

Shadow Man spat and then slapped Theo across his face. "Deny him, you little puke!"

Theo clenched his jaw with the sting of the strike. But that blow jerked him out of his indecision. He spoke the truth of the first seal as if it were the most obvious thing in the world.

"Elyon is the light. Nothing can threaten him."

Shadow Man blinked, taken off guard. "But you aren't," he roared, face red. "You're nothing but a piece of garbage strapped to a pole, blind and rotting! And I *can* threaten you!"

Theo spoke the truth of the second seal. "I am the light. I am the son of Elyon, and you can't threaten me." Heat rose through his chest.

"Lies!" Shadow Man raged in a frenzy. "You're just a boy, a nothing!" He slapped him again. "Deny the light! Deny it now!"

Theo ignored the pain in his jaw and focused on the heat rising in his chest. He didn't need the staff. The light didn't come from the staff. It came from inside of him—he knew that now.

"You're wrong," Theo said. "I *am* the light. I'm the light of the world."

Light drifted from his mouth as he spoke each word, like fog made of sunlight. Shadow Man took one step back, suddenly unsure.

Filled with courage, Theo hurled the words at Shadow Man before he could recover.

"I am the light of the world!" Theo yelled. "You can kill my body and you can blind me all you want, but that doesn't change the truth. I am Elyon's son and I am the light, made like him!"

Light streamed from him now, blinding the Horde, who shrieked and shielded their eyes with their gray hands.

He pressed. "I am the light!"

Annelee joined him. "I am the light of the world!"

The light crackled and swirled around all three posts, vaporizing the ropes holding Theo, Annelee, and Maya as if they'd been made of tissue paper.

Shadow Man's face had gone dark. His teeth clenched and his eyes shifted from blue to red.

"You lie!" A heavy black fog flowed from his mouth.

"I am the light!" Theo cried.

The light surging from Theo, Annelee, and Maya swallowed up Shadow Man's black fog. He threw his hands up to shield his face from that power, but he couldn't stop the light from consuming him.

Theo could hear Annelee and Maya saying something to his right—maybe the second seal too—but the loud roar of the light drowned out their words. It didn't matter.

Shadow Man cowered and shrieked in a pitiful attempt to block the light. His dark power was only a shadow in the face of the light.

Suddenly, Shadow Man stopped his writhing and glared at them, yielding to the light crackling over every inch of his body. His face fell and for a moment he looked terribly sad. Defeated.

His eyes turned deep red and his lips twisted cruelly. "This won't be the last you see of me," he snarled.

Shadow Man's human form vanished, revealing the horrid black beast beneath his skin. He leaped to the sky and streaked away in silence.

Shadow Man was defeated.

He always has been.

The light collapsed into the trio, leaving all three standing alone on the hill next to a crackling bonfire. There was no sign of Ba'al or the other Horde. They'd fled from the light.

For a moment, none of them could speak. Theo's skin buzzed and his insides tingled.

"We did it," Annelee whispered.

"Was there ever any doubt?" Maya said, beaming. "What did I say about Elyon's power?" She pumped her fist in the air. "Nothing can withstand the light. Nothing!"

"Nothing!" Annelee said, laughing. "Nothing at all." She rushed over to Maya and threw her arms around her. "I'm so sorry, Maya. I'm sorry for the way I treated you."

"No need to apologize, Annelee," Maya said, her voice soft and forgiving. "We all take our journeys differently. I'm just glad you see your beauty now, even though you're Horde."

"I'm beautiful, and so are you!"

"Of course I am," Maya said with a giggle.

"Talya said that once I love the one I despise, I would receive the seal. I thought it was you, but really it was me. I've hated myself for a long time, afraid I wasn't beautiful enough."

Theo watched Annelee. He never would have

guessed that Annelee feared not being beautiful enough, but maybe that was true of everyone. It no longer mattered. She knew her true beauty, and it went beyond her costume. That's what mattered.

And he'd found the light without his staff. *He* was the light, not an object that could so easily be destroyed. He was the light because Elyon had made him in his own likeness.

"We must hurry now," Maya said. "Talya told me to take you to the Red Lakes. Follow me."

Theo and Annelee followed their faithful leader through the quiet night of the Horde city and out into the desert. They traveled quickly, not because the Horde guard was chasing them, but because they knew something was calling them.

"Look! There!" Maya raced ahead.

In the distance, Theo recognized a man he knew well—Talya. And by the mystic's side were his three best friends—Michal, Gabil, and Stokes.

They waited beside a pool of water, glistening in the moonlight.

Stokes jumped into the air and did a back flip, thrilled. Theo ran and embraced him.

"Theo, you must tell me everything that happened on your adventure!" Stokes said.

"We must know every detail," Gabil said.

So Theo told them everything, from beginning to end. The Roush hung on each word with many amplified *ooohs* and *ahhhs*. Annelee and Maya joined in, giving their perspectives and adding details he missed.

Talya watched with raised brow, amused.

"And then what?" Stokes asked.

"And then we came here."

"Back here to your protector, the mighty warrior," the little Roush said with a firm nod.

Theo laughed. "If you say so."

Annelee took Talya's old hand in hers and bowed her head.

"Thank you for choosing me to go on this quest with Theo." She lifted the sleeve of the Horde tunic and showed him the two seals on her shoulder. "It's because of you that I met Elyon and now understand the light and beauty inside of me."

Talya patted her hand. "I didn't choose you. The quest chose you. You, just like young Theo, were meant for this quest. But I'm so very glad to hear that you have come to your senses. And when you have all five seals, you will see things in a whole light."

"There are three more?" she said. "How do we get them?"

"That will be for Theo and another."

She glanced at Theo, confused. "What about me?"

"You'll be back, but not for the third seal," Talya said. "Not to worry. When Theo finds the next seal, so will you. You'll see. As for you, brave Theo, be on guard and wait for the next sign. The next seal will be your most difficult thus far. You'll return with someone new."

"Who?"

"When the time comes, you'll know. Ready your heart."

"I will."

"Good," Talya said, turning to the red pool. "And now it's time for you to go home. The red pool will return your skin to what it was before and bring you back to your world. The time has come."

Annelee rubbed her hand down her cracked, gray arm. "I forgot all about my skin."

Theo rubbed his hand on the back of his neck. "Me too."

"Honestly, I wouldn't care if I looked like this forever," she said, winking at Maya. "My skin is only a costume. It doesn't matter what I look like. I'll always be beautiful."

Maya's grin stretched from ear to ear. "But of course!"

"All right, you two, time to say your goodbyes," Talya said.

Annelee and Theo made their rounds, giving hugs and saying goodbye. He wished they didn't have to leave. He wanted more time with his Roush friends. But he knew he'd be back soon.

Theo pretended to tip a hat. "Until next time."

"We will see you soon!" Stokes said.

"Dive into the red pool," Talya instructed. "Let the current take you deep. Breathe the water and it will take you home. There's nothing to be afraid of."

"Breathe it?" Annelee asked.

"It's okay." Theo understood her concern. "I've

done it. It will be like breathing air, or maybe like breathing light. Right, Talya?"

"Something like that, yes." He gestured toward the water. "Go on then. Dive."

Theo took Annelee's hand and stepped up to the pool. "Ready?"

"I guess so."

"Jump!"

They threw themselves out into the pool and were immediately sucked under. Warmth swirled around him. He could live in its comfort forever. Free of fear. Free of worry. He knew Annelee was feeling the same.

He released her hand and let the current pull him deep, deep, and deeper into the pool. The red waters transformed into light, and the light into nothing but air.

Then, by the mystery of Elyon, they were no longer in water but sitting in the upstairs library room, waking from what seemed to be a dream.

But it hadn't been a dream. Not at all.

Annelee stood and stretched. "Wow!" she said.

"Yeah, wow!"

She reached down and helped him off the floor.

Her hand was soft and smooth, void of the Horde disease. He glanced at his arms.

"We're healed!"

"I . . . I can't believe that happened," she said, feeling the backs of her hands.

"What did I tell you? It's amazing, isn't it?"

He could finally talk to someone on this side. Annelee White—the girl of his dreams—was no longer the new girl he had been afraid to talk to for the past six years. She was his friend.

"What?" she asked with a giggle. "Why are you staring at me?"

He was staring? "Oh! Nothing. Just happy to have a friend to share this with."

Annelee hugged him and he forgot to breathe. "More than just a friend."

She pulled back and lifted the sleeve of her dress. The white and green circles glowed in the dim room. He shoved his sleeve up and revealed his seals too—a matching pair of green and white.

"Will everyone be able to see these? I don't think my mom would be too thrilled if she thought her twelve-year-old daughter got tatted up."

"We're the only ones who can see them."

"Cool." Concern passed over her face. "Oh no! What time is it?"

"I don't know. Time acts funny between the two worlds. We've probably only been gone for an hour or less, but it could be more."

"The dance!" Annelee cried.

They ran to the door, hurried out of the room, and peeked over the railing at the library below. Mrs. Friend was still at her desk.

Theo headed down the stairs with Annelee close behind.

"Well, you two were up there for a while. Must have been some story. You get lost in another world?"

How could she know?

"I guess we did," Annelee said, smiling at Theo.

"I'm sure you did. Well, you two better hurry up, that dance is about to start. Guess I can lock up now."

He followed Annelee toward the door, then turned back. "Mrs. Friend?"

"Yes?"

"Thank you for telling me . . . us about the room."

She winked at him. "Our secret. Now that she's seen the book, we'll say it belongs to both of you. Sound good?"

He didn't know what Mrs. Friend knew, but it sure seemed like she knew more about that book than she'd told him.

"Yes, ma'am."

Theo and Annelee ran out of the library doors, filled with the wonder of the quest and the seals on their arms. Something big was happening in their lives. And it wasn't over, not by a long shot.

They came to a quick stop when they noticed Asher Brox walking down the hall. Theo pulled Annelee behind the corner. Asher hadn't seen them, but he dreaded what would happen if he did.

Annelee whispered, "We are the light. Remember? No fear."

She grabbed his hand and dashed down the hallway, passing Asher like a blur. He yelled something at them, but they didn't hear it. They rounded the corner and crashed through the gym doors.

The room was full of music and lights. Students were already dancing. No one even noticed they'd entered.

Annelee pulled Theo onto the dance floor.

"Wait! I can't dance!" he said.

"Theo Dunnery, we are the light of the world! Surely, the light can dance, even if it looks silly to the rest of the world!"

She was right. So he danced a dance he never knew he could dance.

With Annelee at his side, nothing could stop him.

CONTINUE THE QUEST!

The DREAM TRAVELER'S QUEST

~3~

THE GARDEN
AND
THE SERPENT

TED DEKKER
KARA DEKKER